AT THE Aquarium

CLEVER CREATURES

by
Mignonne Gunasekara

BEARPORT PUBLISHING

Minneapolis, Minnesota

PHOTO CREDITS

All images are courtesy of Shutterstock.com, unless otherwise specified. With thanks to Getty Images, Thinkstock Photo and iStockphoto.Plant Vectors Throughout – Baksiabat, MicroOne. Front Cover – Oksana Golubeva, Konstantin Novikov, Damsea, Rich Carey, Gaidamashchuk. 4–5 – Rich Carey. 6–7 – Jason Mintze, Gabriele Maltinti, Martin Voeller, Kondratuk Aleksei, fredrisher. 8–9 – Gerald Robert Fischer, acro_phuket, Kim David. 10–11 – Bildagentur Zoonar GmbH, small1, Focused Adventures, fredrisher. 12–13 – Rich Carey, Jolanta Wojcicka, fredrisher. 14–15 – UnderTheSea, Bence Sibalin, stephan kerkhofs, Andre Silva Pinto, Nadzin. 16–17 – Ethan Daniels, John A. Anderson, Vlad61. 18–19 – Richard Whitcombe, Bence Sibalin, Daniel Poloha. 20–21 – Vilmos Varga, UnderTheSea, Maksimilian. 22–23 – blue-sea.cz, Rich Carey, Rawpixel.com.

Library of Congress Cataloging-in-Publication Data is available at www.loc.gov or upon request from the publisher.

ISBN: 978-1-64747-403-4 (hardcover)
ISBN: 978-1-64747-410-2 (paperback)
ISBN: 978-1-64747-417-1 (ebook)

For more information, write to Bearport Publishing, 5357 Penn Avenue South, Minneapolis, MN 55419.
Printed in the United States of America.

CONTENTS

WELCOME TO THE AQUARIUM!

Welcome to the aquarium! Aquariums look after sea animals. Many aquariums do lots of work to protect wild animals, too.

Let's look at some sea creatures that aren't like other fish.

Let's meet eight clever creatures!

GIANT PACIFIC OCTOPUS

The giant Pacific octopus uses the suckers on its eight arms to hold things. It can even open jars!

The giant Pacific octopus is the largest type of octopus on Earth.

These octopuses can change their color to blend in with what is around them. This helps them hide from **predators** and catch **prey.**

This octopus eats shrimp, lobsters, and fish.

Giant Pacific octopuses hunt at night.

PEACOCK MANTIS SHRIMP

The peacock mantis shrimp lives in warm waters.

The peacock mantis shrimp has a hard shell. It gets its name from the bright blue and green colors on the male shrimp's shell.

Peacock mantis shrimps have a secret weapon. They are small, but they have a club-like claw that packs a very powerful punch.

This shrimp's punch is so strong that it can break through glass!

The powerful punch can crack the shells of snails and crabs.

JAPANESE SPIDER CRAB

The Japanese spider crab is the largest crab on Earth.

The Japanese spider crab is also known as the giant crab. It spends most of its time deep underwater near the country of Japan.

Japanese spider crabs eat both plants and other animals. They will even eat dead animals.

Japanese spider crabs can live to be 100 years old!

When stretched out, the tips of their claws can be 13 feet (4 m) apart!

BANDED SEA KRAIT

The banded sea krait is a sea snake.

Banded sea kraits live near **coral** reefs. They have paddle-shaped tails that help them swim.

Banded sea kraits eat mostly eels. Their predators are seabirds.

This snake's bite is filled with **venom**.

Banded sea kraits can hold their breath underwater for up to 2 hours!

GIANT CLAM

Algae share the food they make with the clams.

Giant clams live in warm, **shallow** water. **Algae** that live in the clams make food from sunlight.

Giant clams are giant! They can weigh up to 500 pounds (227 kg).

GROOVED BRAIN CORAL

The center of a grooved brain coral is a hard skeleton. The grooves on the outside hold the living part of the coral.

The grooved brain coral got its name because it looks like a brain!

Grooved brain corals grow in shallow water. They need lots of sunlight.

The grooved brain coral gets food from the algae that live on it.

The small animals that are the living part of the coral on the outside are called **polyps**.

CROWN-OF-THORNS STARFISH

If a crown-of-thorns starfish loses an arm, it can grow the arm back.

Crown-of-thorns starfish live on coral reefs. They eat by turning their stomachs inside out and eating the polyps off coral skeletons.

These starfish are covered in spines. The spines contain venom that keeps most predators away.

The giant sea snail is the starfish's main predator. It is not scared away by the starfish's spines.

ACORN BARNACLE

Acorn barnacles have hard shells to protect their soft bodies.

Acorn barnacles attach themselves to hard things, such as rocks, or even animals, such as whales!

The acorn barnacle catches food with a special leg. It sticks the leg out of an opening at the top of its shell to grab food.

After a barnacle attaches to something, it cannot move.

Acorn barnacles eat **plankton**.

THANKS FOR VISITING!

Many of the animals we learned about in this book call coral reefs home.

Thank you for stopping by the aquarium. If you like clever creatures, there are things you can do to keep them safe.

Garbage in the ocean is a big problem for coral reefs. We all need to do our best to keep the ocean clean.

Throw away your trash and recycle what you can. This helps keep the ocean clean!

GLOSSARY

algae tiny plantlike living things that grow in water

coral a group of rocklike structures made from the skeletons of sea animals also called coral

plankton tiny animals and plants that float in water

polyps sea animals, such as coral, that have tentacles and a round mouth

predators animals that hunt other animals for food

prey animals that are hunted by other animals for food

shallow not deep

venom a harmful substance that is injected through a bite or a sting

INDEX